THE RAINBOW
AND
THE RED DRAGON

MARY DONNA HANKLA

MARY DONNA HANKLA

Printed Worldwide
First Printing 2025
First Edition 2025

ISBN: 979-8-9925029-2-3

Library of Congress Control Number: 2025922653

10 9 8 7 6 5 4 3 2 1

Book Cover by Hmdpublishing @hmdgfx

THE RAINBOW
AND
THE RED DRAGON

TABLE OF CONTENTS

DEDICATION

One main purpose of this book is to reveal the protective power of God.

Even as the rainbow surrounds God's Throne; we are surrounded by His protection.

Yes, there are spiritual enemies and human enemies, but God has a hedge of protection around us; even as Job experienced.

Satan admitted that he not could touch Job because of this Divine Hedge of Protection (Job 1:10).

Certain people surround me in prayer and with encouragement. They are ready to assist at a moment's notice. This book is dedicated to those who truly stand with me.

My husband, Kenneth Hankla, has stood with me numerous years, and I trust that we will enjoy many more years together. He is a support of prayer and he is quick to encourage me.

Christopher Mark Hankla is a son of great faith. He loves God and serves in the ministry with excellence. His encouragement keeps me writing and his computer skills are vital to the completion of each book.

Bill and Kaveda are our neighbors. Words cannot express the amount of prayer and support that they provide. Not only do they encourage the writing of books, but they also promote our Big 4 P.H. Church You - Tube programs. When they pray, God's

Presence can be felt. There is power in their prayers!

Also, I appreciate my niece, Katrina Shefield. She assures me that my books are helpful. She is an encourager.

Finally, I continue to appreciate Ron and Sandra Fowler of South Carolina. For many years they have prayed for our family and ministry.

INTRODUCTION

What could a rainbow and a red dragon possibly have in common? The answer is found in the book of Revelation!

Both play a pivotal role in the Book of Revelation and the end times events.

A spectacular rainbow surrounds the Throne of God. The Apostle John observed this phenomenon during his tour of the Throne of Heaven (Revelation Chapter 4).

The rainbow is noted to be a promise of God made to Noah in regards to the Great Flood.

And God said, "This is the token (visible, symbol, memorial) of the (solemn) covenant which I am making between Me and you and every living creature that is with you, for all future generations."

I set My rainbow in the clouds, and it shall be a sign of a covenant between Me and the earth."

It shall come about, when I bring clouds over the earth, that the rainbow shall be seen in the clouds.

And I will (compassionately) remember My covenant, which is between Me and you and every living creature of all flesh; and never again will the water become a flood to destroy all flesh.

When the rainbow is in the clouds and I look at it, I will (solemnly) remember the everlasting covenant between God and every living creature of all flesh that is on the earth"

(Genesis 9: 12 – 16) (The Amplified Study Bible).

The rainbow is a well-known promise of the Divine. However, it is much more. It is also a weapon against the Red Dragon.

When we see a rainbow, our hearts are filled with hope and joy. However, when the Devil sees the rainbow around God's Throne, he sees a heavenly weapon that emits defensive rays against God's enemies!

God's Throne is shielded by the rainbow and other creatures.

Prayer Lessons Taught from the Rainbow

The rainbow surrounding God's Throne has much to teach about effective prayer.

God's Word speaks of resisting the devil. James 4:7 reads, "We are to resist the devil and he will flee from us."

But how exactly are we to resist the Devil? Prayer is our main method of resisting the devil, especially prayers that pray God's Word! These prayers send the devil fleeing!

Consider the time that Jesus was tempted in the wilderness by the devil. He continued to quote God's Word, and finally commanded the devil to flee.

"Then Jesus said to him, "Go away, Satan! For it is written and forever remains written, "You shall worship the Lord Your God, and serve Him only."

"Then the devil left Him; and angels came and ministered to Him (bringing Him food and serving Him) (Matthew 4: 10,11).

Scriptural prayers are effective in two ways.

1. They send the devil fleeing.
2. They open doors for angels to intervene in our battles.

A few key prayer lessons taught by the rainbow include:

1. God is faithful, even during storms of life. The rainbow symbolizes His faithfulness.

2. Trusting God is also noted. The rainbow brings renewed hope after the storm.

   - "Trust (rely on and have confidence) in the Lord and do good" (Psalm 37: 3).

3. Mercy is given by God even during times of judgment.

   - "In wrath (earnestly) remember compassion" (Habakkuk 3:2). This is a prayer of the prophet.

4. Connecting with God is also a rainbow prayer promise. Even as the Rainbow that surrounds God's Throne is connected, we too can enjoy His Presence. For the rainbow is within

God's sight, and so are we! (Revelation 4:3).

5. The rainbow surrounds God's Throne. It circles the Throne. We are also surrounded by God's favor and protection.

"For You, O Lord, bless the righteous man (the one who is in right standing with You): You surround him with favor as a shield" (Psalm 5:12).

Jesus encouraged prayers for protection when He taught the disciples The Lord's Prayer.

"And do not lead us into temptation, but deliver us from evil" (Matthew 6: 13).

War in Heaven

The scene painted in Revelation 12 is one of the most dramatic moments in all of Scripture. Imagine the heavens shaking as the forces of light and darkness collide.

Michael, the mighty archangel of God, steps forward, not with hesitation but with the authority of the One he serves. Behind him stands an army of angels, ready to defend the holiness of God's throne. Against them rises the red dragon, Satan, and his horde of fallen spirits.

This was no minor skirmish. It was a cosmic war, a battle that determined the fate of eternity. The Scripture tells us plainly: *"And war broke out in heaven, Michael and his angels waging war with the dragon. The dragon and his angels fought, but they were not strong enough, and there was no longer a place found for them in heaven"* (Revelation 12:7–8).

The outcome was never in question. Darkness can never overpower light. The dragon, called the devil and Satan, was thrown down, cast out from the presence of God, his rebellion crushed. His deception had no foothold in the courts of heaven. His pride found no place among the righteous. His lies could not endure before the truth. *"He who continually deceives and seduces the entire inhabited world was thrown down to the earth, and his angels were thrown down with him"* (Revelation 12:9).

Why Was There War in Heaven?

What could cause such conflict in the very presence of God? The answer is sobering: pride. Satan was not content with the honor given to him. He was once the anointed cherub, clothed in splendor, walking among the fiery stones of God's holy mountain. He had beauty, wisdom, and authority, yet he desired more.

Discontentment grew into ambition, and ambition into rebellion. He wanted not only to serve before God's throne but to sit upon it. He desired the worship that belongs to God alone. Though he was created, he craved the status of the Creator.

Ezekiel reminds us of his former glory: *"You were the anointed cherub who covers and protects, and I placed you there; you were on the holy mountain of God; you walked in the midst of the stones of fire"* (Ezekiel 28:14). And yet, he despised the position God had given him. That dissatisfaction festered until war was the only outcome.

Sin Began in His Heart

Rebellion often starts in the same place: the **HEART**. Before Satan ever raised his voice in defiance, before he gathered angels to his cause, pride was planted deep within him. It began as a whisper of desire: *"I will ascend. I will rise above. I will make myself like the Most High."*

Isaiah records his words: *"But you said in your heart, 'I will ascend to heaven; I will raise my throne above the stars of God; I will sit on the mount of assembly in the remote parts of the north. I will ascend above the heights of the clouds; I will make myself like the Most High'"* (Isaiah 14:13–14).

Notice that sin did not start in his hands but in his heart. What begins as pride in the unseen places eventually pours out into rebellion that can be seen by all. The fall of Satan reminds us that sin unchecked will always grow, and pride left unchallenged will always destroy.

King David Prays

Centuries later, King David understood the same truth. The battle for holiness is not fought first in the public arena but in the hidden chambers of the heart. When he sinned, he didn't begin his prayer by asking for restored reputation or renewed honor. He cried out for something deeper: a clean heart.

"Behold, You desire truth in the innermost being, and in the hidden part You will make me know wisdom. Purify me with hyssop, and I will be clean; wash me, and I will be whiter than snow. Make me hear joy and gladness and be satisfied" (Psalm 51:6–8).

David teaches us that sin corrupts from within, and only God can cleanse at that level. His most famous plea still echoes across time: *"Create in me a clean heart, O God, and renew a right and steadfast spirit within me"* (Psalm 51:10).

David's prayer is a safeguard against the very downfall that consumed Satan. Pride whispers, "I will ascend," but humility cries, "Lord, purify me." Pride reaches for God's throne, but humility kneels before it. David shows us the way to remain in right standing with God starts with the heart.

CHAPTER 1: THE RAGE OF THE RED DRAGON

The Book of Revelation is truly fascinating. It begins with a Glorious Vision of Jesus Christ (Ch. 1). It proceeds with Jesus speaking personal messages to each of the seven churches. Then, John the Apostle, is given a tour of the Throne Room of Heaven (Revelation 4). The Book continues with the Seal Judgments, the Trumpet Judgments and the Bowl Judgments. It concludes with a view of the New Jerusalem and New Earth.

The War Waged by the Red Dragon

Angels and demons were engaged in a fierce fight. Archangel Michael led the angels in the battle. The demons followed the commands of the Great Red Dragon.

John the Apostle was given a vision of the war. This event is called a *warning*.

"Then another sign of (warning) was seen in heaven: behold a great fiery red dragon (Satan) with seven heads and ten horns, and on his heads were seven royal crowns (diadems)."

"And his tail swept (across the sky) and dragged away a third of the stars of heaven and flung them to the earth. And the dragon stood in front of the woman who was about to give birth, so that when she gave birth he might devour her child" (Revelation 12: 3,4).

The Red Dragon is also known to be the devil. His red color reflects his murderous nature. The seven heads and seven crowns emphasize the completeness and universality of his power.

The Red Dragon is a personification of a triad of evil spirits; namely the witchcraft spirit, the religious spirit and the Jezebel spirit. These spirits operated through flesh to nail Jesus to the cross. The religious spirit viciously attacked Jesus with false accusations (Luke 23:8 -12).

The devil and his hordes of demons were no match for Archangel Michael and his hosts of angels.

The devil and the demons that followed him were cast from heaven.

"And war broke out in heaven, Michael (the archangel) and his angels waging war with the dragon. The dragon and his angels fought,

But they were not strong enough and did not prevail, and there was no longer a place found for them in heaven" (Revelation 12:7,8).

The vision begins with a woman clothed with the sun, and the moon under her feet, and upon her head a crown of 12 stars. She is pregnant and is suffering pains of labor. During her agony, the great Red Dragon lashes out. He stands awaiting the birth of the child, so that he might devour this child (Revelation 12:3-4).

It is suggested that the woman represents the nation of Israel, while the child refers to Jesus Christ.

During the vision, the Apostle John saw heavenly help provided to the woman so that she could escape the wrath of the devil. She was given two wings like an eagle to flee from the enemy.

When the devil saw that he could not harm the woman or child, he went forth to wage

war with the remnant of her seed
(Revelation 12:17).

Do Not Ignore

Yes, this Red Dragon is the ancient serpent
who was kicked out of heaven because of
pride and rebellion. He is known by several
titles:

- The Devil
- The Tempter
- Beelzebul
- The god of this world
- The adversary
- The accuser
- The father of lies

The Apostle John uses a strong word prior
to describing the Red Dragon.

He says to BEHOLD! In the Bible this word
means to observe or notice something of

importance. It suggests that something noteworthy is about to occur.

Again, a mention is made of the color red for this dragon. He is described as fiery red which is known as the color of warfare.

The main theme of Revelation is the spiritual warfare that the devil wages against God's people.

It is an invisible warfare, and be assured that the enemy lurks around seeking those whom he may devour (I Peter 5:8).

The devil and his demons are watching for an opportune time to strike. Recall the temptation of Jesus in the wilderness. After three unsuccessful attempts, the devil left Jesus and waited for a more opportune time to attack.

"When the devil had finished every temptation, he (temporarily) left Him until a more opportune time" (Luke 4: 13).

Many people suffer needlessly from sudden attacks of the devil. Yet they chose to ignore the devil and brush off the attacks.

However, to ignore the devil is to fall prey to him. There are several reasons not to ignore the Red Dragon.

*You will never withstand the wiles of the devil by ignoring him.

*You can never escape the fangs of a lion by turning a deaf ear.

*You may desire to run from the devil, or ignore him, but both choices incite him to pursue you.

*It is better to know the enemy who picks a fight. You must be able to see this enemy and discern his plans of evil. This way you can be one step ahead of the adversary.

"So submit to (the authority of) God. Resist the devil (stand firm against him) and he will flee from you" (James 4:7)

Two Weapons

The devil is portrayed as an accuser of the brethren, and as a murderer.

However, he is defeated by the blood of Jesus and the word of our testimony (Revelation 12: 11).

Personal Demonic Attacks

I have experienced some dramatic demonic attacks. These evil attacks knocked me down at times. But I would quickly enter my prayer closet and ask for wisdom. The wisdom of God has delivered me from the hand of the evil many times!

Consider the Wisdom of Jesus! There was a group of people who tried to set a trap for Jesus so they could accuse Him.

"Then they sent some of the Pharisees and Herodians to Jesus (in order to trap Him into

making a statement (that they could use against Him" (Mark 12: 13).

They used the theme of taxes for their bait. Should they pay taxes to Caesar or not?

"Should we pay (the tax) or should we not pay? But knowing their hypocrisy, He asked them, "Why are you testing Me? Bring me a coin (denarius) to look at" (Mark 12: 15).

"So they brought one. Then He asked them, "Whose image and inscription is this? They said to Him, "Caesar's" (Mark 12: 16).

"Jesus said to them, "Pay unto Caesar the things that are Caesar's and to God the things that are God's." And they were greatly amazed at Him" (Mark 12:17).

Wisdom is Truly an Effective Weapon!

Jesus taught His disciples about wisdom.

"Listen carefully: I am sending you out like sheep among wolves; so be wise as serpents, and innocent as doves (have no self-serving agenda)" (Matthew 10: 16.)

Other lessons learned are to appropriate the Blood of Jesus by prayer and to speak the Word of God over your battles!

Recall the time that the Israelites were told to apply the Blood of the Lamb on their doorposts.

By doing this, they essentially placed a spiritual hedge of protection over themselves and their household.

"The blood shall be a sign for you on (the doorposts of) the houses where you live; when I see the blood I shall pass over you, and no affliction shall happen to you to destroy you when I strike the land of Egypt" (Exodus 12: 13).

Finally, I have learned that trials do eventually end. My actions can shorten the time of the trial if I use wisdom.

Many people become discouraged because they are worn down by the trial. But after the trial God promises to strengthen us.

"After you have suffered for a little while, the God of all grace (who imparts His blessing and favor), who called you to His own eternal glory in Christ, will Himself complete, confirm, strengthen, and establish you (making you what you ought to be) (I Peter 5: 10).

She Swung Her Fist Toward my Head

One particular episode of spiritual warfare that happened to me was at a job site.

I worked as a Chaplain and a nurse. I visited the sick, helped with hospice, and preached in the Chapel each Sunday.

One lady constantly opposed me. Every day, she tried to set me up for failure. But I ignored her. I was enthralled with the joy of ministering to needy people. Every day was a reward for me, because I was able to help someone, listen to their concerns and pray with them.

One morning I approached the time clock and clocked in for work. Just as soon as I turned around, this person rushed toward me! In a flash, she threw a round-house swing with her fist directly towards my head!

Fortunately, I ducked and she missed. Then, she left the scene.

I was appalled to experience something like this at work. Thankfully, despite the shock of the situation, I was able to regain my composure and continue my day.

God had protected me and I was not harmed!

I believe that divine protection was released on my behalf due to my morning prayers. I have a habit of starting my day with prayer, and I find great power in praying the scriptures!

Verses of divine protection which I pray frequently are found in Psalm 91.

"Because you have made the Lord, (who is) my refuge, Even the Most High, your dwelling place.

"NO EVIL WILL BEFALL YOU."

Nor will any plague come near your tent" (Psalm 91: 9,10).

Blue Lights Flashing

It seems that the devil launches evil attacks when we travel to church.

Generally, it is a small attack, such as someone calling with a complaint.

However, one evening my friend and I were traveling to a church camp meeting. We were excited about the worship program on the schedule as well as the guest speakers.

I was driving and we were discussing some of the great things that God had done in our lives.

Our joy was short-lived. We heard a siren and looked behind us. A state police car was following us and urging us to pull over.

The traffic was heavy, and I had a hard time finding a place to pull over.

When the officer approached my car, I noticed that he was very young. I asked him why he pulled me over.

You will never guess the response that he gave.

"You were traveling 5 miles below the speed limit. The speed limit is 65 miles an hour. Your speed was 60 miles an hour."

I stayed calm and told him that I would go before the court with this charge.

When the court date came, my friend testified on my behalf. The charge for driving too slow was dropped.

Fear and accusation were two of the evil weapons aimed at me.

As I prepared myself for the court date, I searched the scriptures for answers.

The following scripture gave me the confidence that I needed to remain in peace during the court session.

"For God did not give us a spirit of timidity or cowardice or fear, but (He has given us a spirit) of power and of love and of sound judgment, and personal discipline (abilities that result in a calm, well- balanced mind and self-control) (II Timothy 1:7).

Jesus demonstrated the power of remaining in peace during a storm.

The Book of Mark tells us of a time when Jesus and His disciples were sailing on the sea in the evening.

"On that (same) day, when evening had come, He said to them, "Let us go over to the other side (of the Sea of Galilee)" (Mark 4:35).

A fierce storm arose, the wind blew with great force, and water rushed onto the boat.

In distress, the disciples woke Jesus. He had been sleeping in the stern.

Jesus got up and addressed the storm with words of authority.

"And He got up and (sternly) rebuked the wind and said to the sea, "Hush, be still (muzzled)!" And the wind died down (as if it had grown weary) and there was (at once) a great calm (a perfect peacefulness)" (Mark 4: 39).

The peace of Jesus stopped a destructive storm!

I will end this testimony with a scripture that has calmed me during many difficult times. I find that when I pray this scripture, fear leaves me and peace flows into my heart and my mind.

"That You may grant him (power to calm himself and find) peace in the days of adversity" (Psalm 94: 13).

Witchcraft

The Great Red Dragon is the inspiration for witchcraft of all types.

Witchcraft is the use of supernatural power and gifts without the source of The Holy Spirit.

Basically, two powers exist. The power of God is available for those who submit their lives to the Lord. Some of the gifts of The Holy Spirit include:

"And there are (distinctive) ways of working (to accomplish things), but it is the same God who produces all things in all believers (inspiring, energizing, and empowering them)" (I Corinthians 12: 6).

"To one is given through the (Holy) Spirit (the power to speak) the message of wisdom, and to another (the power to express) the word of knowledge and understanding according to the same Spirit" (I Corinthians 12: 8).

"to another (wonder-working) faith (is given) by the same (Holy) Spirit, and to another the extraordinary gifts of healings by one Spirit" (I Corinthians 12: 9).

Other gifts of the Holy Spirit include:

- Working of miracles
- The gift of prophecy
- The gift of discernment of spirits

The Great Red Dragon is also known as the age-old serpent, the Devil and Satan (Revelation 12: 9).

He also offers supernatural gifts that spring from the source of the evil one.

Some of these satanic gifts include:

- Divination as seen in Acts 16: 1-13
- Sorcery ---- Simon the Sorcerer is mentioned in Acts 8: 9 -24
- Necromancy ---- the practice of communicating with the dead. Recall King Saul consulting the dead by a witch. (I Samuel 28)
- Cartomancy--- divination by use of Tarot cards
- Witchcraft with stars --- (Deuteronomy 4:19)

Testimonies of former witches make mention of these gifts and many more.

One particular gift they have in common is astral projection. This is the demonic supernatural ability to separate from their physical bodies and travel to places of innocent victims for the purpose of releasing evil curses.

Sorcery

Sorcery is also an evil gift that springs from the Great Red Dragon.

Some practices that sorcery comprises are:

*Deception is a strong tool of sorcery.

*Through the use of deception, the sorcerer attempts to gain power, to manipulate, and to control.

*Divination is also associated with sorcery.

*Releasing spells and incantations are also associated with sorcery.

*Another practice of sorcery is necromancy.

*Finally, witchcraft, with the desire to control is often seen with acts of sorcery.

Barnabas and Saul encountered a sorcerer when they traveled to the region of Salamis (Acts 13: 5 – 12).

They were hindered by a sorcerer known as Elymas.

The apostles were preaching the Gospel to the people of the region.

A government leader was very receptive to the message and wanted to accept Jesus as Savior, but Elymas was determined to block the salvation of this government leader.

"But Elymas the sorcerer (for that is how his name is translated) opposed them, trying to turn the proconsul away from accepting the faith" (Acts 13: 8).

*"But Saul, who was also known as Paul, filled with the Holy Spirit and led by Him, looked steadily at Elymas" *Acts 13: 9).*

Paul addressed the sorcerer sternly and exposed his true goals:

"and said, "You (Elymas) who are full of every (kind) of deceit, and every (kind of) fraud, you son of the devil, enemy of everything that is right and good, will you never stop perverting the straight paths of the Lord?" (Acts 13: 10).

Paul continued with strong words, declaring that Elymas would be blind, not able to see the sun for a time (season) (Acts 13: 11).

Immediately a mist of darkness fell upon him, and he groped around. He sought for someone to lead him by the hand (Acts 13: 11).

The Great Red Dragon has no might against the Spirit of God, the Word of God, or the Blood of Jesus!

Defeat of the Red Dragon

The defeat of the Red Dragon in your life can start today. If Jesus lives in your heart because you accepted Him, then you have the upper hand.

Recall that Satan is also called the god of this world, but victory belongs to those who are born of God.

"For everyone born of God is victorious and overcomes the world; and this is the victory that has conquered and overcome the world— our (continuing, persistent) faith (in Jesus the Son of God)"

(I John 5: 4).

Scripture continues to confirm our victory with the next verse.

"Who is the one who is victorious and overcomes the world? It is the one who believes and recognizes the fact that Jesus is the Son of God" (I John 5: 5).

The Red Dragon fears the name of Jesus, the blood of Jesus, and your faith!

The Threat of the Rainbow

For those who follow Jesus, this rainbow is a symbol of victory!

But for the Great Red Dragon and his followers the rainbow around the Throne of God is a reminder of their eternal defeat.

"And He who sat there appeared like (the crystalline sparkle of) a jasper stone and (the fiery redness of) a sardius stone, and encircling the throne there was a RAINBOW that looked like (the color of an emerald (Revelation 4: 3).

There are three reasons that this rainbow reminds the devil of his defeat.

1.   The rainbow is a symbol that God has established a coventant of protection for His people.

- Recall God placing the rainbow in the sky for Noah to see after the flood.
- "And God said, "This is the token (visible symbol, memorial) of the (solemn) covenant which I am making between Me and you and every living creature that is with you, for all future generations" (Genesis 9: 12).
- This covenant was extended to future generations!

2. The faithfulness of God to His people is seen with the rainbow. God is faithful to defend His people from the evil dragon.

- When God sees the rainbow He is reminded of His promises to His people.
- "When the rainbow is in the clouds and I look at it, I will

solemnly remember the everlasting covenant between God and every living creature of all flesh that is on the earth" (Genesis 9:16).

3. Reassurance is a third threat to the devil. The rainbow reminds God's people that He has defeated the devil.

    *   The rainbow confirms to the devil that he was defeated when Jesus died and rose again from the dead!
    *   Proof of this statement, is seen by the flood sent by God in the days of Noah.
    *   This flood destroyed all the wicked which opposed God.
    *   There is a scripture that reassures us that The Great Red Dragon has been disarmed and defeated!
    *   "When He disarmed the rulers and authorities (those supernatural forces of evil

operating against us), He made a public example of them (exhibiting them as captives in His triumphal procession, having triumphed over them through the cross" (Colossians 2: 15).

Reflection Questions

The Apostle John was wisked up to heaven and witnessed life-changing scenes.

This is a challenge for you, the reader, to study Revelation Chapter 4. As you read the scenes of heaven, take time to envision each tour station.

These questions will help you grasp the majesty of heaven.

1. Who was the first person that John saw?
2. Describe the throne that John saw.
3. Imagine the rainbow encircling the throne (Revelation 4: 3).

4. How does this Heavenly Rainbow compare with rainbows you have seen on earth?

5. What do you sense when you read about flashes of lightening and sounds of thunder surrounding the throne?

6. Finally, what are the Seven Spirits of God that burn in front of the throne? (Revelation 4: 5) (Isaiah 11).

CHAPTER 2: MYSTERIES OF THE RAINBOW SURROUNDING GOD'S THRONE

Rainbows are marvels of nature that inspire us. Not every rainbow is the same. Some rainbows appear as a double rainbow, other rainbows radiate brilliant colors, but all rainbows are incredible.

Rainbows ignite hope in the eyes of many. Viewing a beautiful rainbow holds deep significance for those who discover them.

Rainbows are rich in symbolism for multiple religions and cultural beliefs. Simply put, rainbows brighten your day!

The Third Heaven and the First Heaven

Rainbows can be seen in both the Third Heaven and the First Heaven.

The First Heaven consists of the earthly realm. The rainbow that appeared after Noah's Ark landed on safe ground is a prime example.

A rainbow in the Third Heaven is seen encircling God's Throne. The Apostle John saw this rainbow and described its sovereign purpose!

He described the rainbow as radiating the color of an emerald and encircling God's Throne (Revelation 4: 3).

Between the Third Heaven and the First Heaven lies the Second Heaven. It is in this atmosphere that many spiritual battles are frequently fought.

According to Ephesians 6:12, the Second Heaven comprises of principalities of evil in the heavenly realms.

The Apostle Paul provides insight regarding the levels of heaven.

"I know a man in Christ who fourteen years ago---whether in the body I do not know, or out of the body I do not know, (only) God knows---such a man was caught up into the third heaven" (II Corinthians 12: 2).

It appears that this man experienced a significant heavenly encounter, hearing heavenly words.

"was caught up into Paradise and heard inexpressible words which man is not permitted

to speak (words to sacred to tell)" (II
Corinthians 12: 4).

In regards to the Second Heaven,
confirmation is found in the Book of
Daniel.

Daniel was informed about a heavenly war
that delayed his prayers. Both angels and
demons were engaged in warfare.
Principalities of powers were demonstrating
their domain over certain regions.

Recall that Daniel had been fasting and
praying prior to receiving a message from an
angel.

His prayers and fastings were credited for
bringing forth heavenly assistance.

"Then he said to me, "Do not be afraid,
Daniel, for from the first day that you set your
heart on understanding this and on humbling
yourself before your God, your words were

heard, and I have come for your words"
(Daniel 10: 12).

Next the angel explained that spiritual warfare was waging in the heavenlies. Because of this warfare, the angel had been hindered in his mission to answer Daniel's prayers.

"But the prince of the kingdom of Persia was standing in opposition to me for twenty-one days. Then, behold, Michael, one of the chief (of celestial) princes, came to help me, for I had been left there with the kings of Persia"
(Daniel 10: 13).

More detailed descriptions of the warfare are provided in this same chapter:

"But I (Gabriel) will tell you what is inscribed in the writing of this truth. There is no one who stands firmly with me and strengthens himself against (these hostile spirit forces) except Michael, your prince (the guardian of your nation)" (Daniel 10: 21).

The Rainbow is a Symbol of Victory for All Heavens!

When God's people view a rainbow, they are encouraged by God's promises. Their faith is strengthened!

When the demons see a rainbow, they are reminded that God's protection encircles His people. They are also reminded that Satan and many of his angels were cast out of heaven!

Jesus told His disciples that He had witnessed the fall of Satan:

"He said to them, "I watched Satan fall from heaven like (a flash of) lightening" (Luke 10: 18).

I Heard the Angels Sing

Even though I was not in heaven, I heard angels singing in a heavenly language.

Hearing a heavenly choir of angels sing was a game-changer for me.

This experience was also recorded in my first book: IN YOUR LIGHT WE SEE LIGHT.

The significance of this event relates to a period of time of corporate prayer meetings with churches in Bluefield, WV.

I believe that this time period of about 18 months, during which I was engaged in corporate prayers with other churches, opened the doors of heaven. During this time period, I received several heavenly encounters!

One morning I went to the Voice of Praise Church in Bluefield, WV. I was sitting in the lobby, waiting for a meeting with the Pastor. There was nobody else in the Church. Suddenly, I heard very loud singing coming from the sanctuary!

I noted the time to be 9:00 a.m. I remembered that this was the start of an important prayer watch seen in both the Old and New Testaments. This is also known as the Sixth Watch. It ranges from 9:00 a.m. to 12:00 p.m.

One famous event that happened during this prayer watch was the out-pouring of the Holy Spirit which descended upon the heads of those present in the form of fire (Acts 2:3 and 15).

Who could be singing at this time of day? It could not be the church choir for they practiced at night. Also, the lights were turned off in the sanctuary!

Being curious, I ventured into the sanctuary. There was a very bright light shining at the top of the sanctuary, just a few feet from the right side of the pulpit. The light illuminated a large portion of the ceiling.

In this area of light, I heard several angels singing. I could not see the angels, but I could sense their presence.

The angelic singing was not in English, Latin, or Spanish. It was not in any earthly language!

The angels did not seem to be hindered by my presence. They sang loud and with intense joy!

I could feel joy! I could feel peace!

The angels were focused on their worship. Even as they sang, a wind of the Holy Spirit blew through the room.

I recalled a scripture passage from the Book of Job.

"When the morning stars sang together, and all the sons of God shouted for joy" (Job 38:7).

Two Things Learned

The angelic singing taught me two major lessons.

First, angels are active performing God's Word. That is why I pray *scriptural prayers.*

"Bless the Lord, you His angels, You mighty ones who do His commandments, obeying the voice of His word (Psalm 103: 20).

The second thing that I understood from this experience is the fact that angels are ministering spirits.

"Are not all the angels ministering spirits sent out (by God) to serve (accompany, protect) those who will inherit salvation? (Of course they are!) (Hebrews 1: 14)

Colors of the Rainbow

Go back with me to your 4th grade science class. Most of us took a course called Earth Science.

We learned that the rainbow gets its colors from water droplets that perform like prisms.

Sunlight and rain in the atmosphere work together to create a rainbow.

The following steps will give understanding of the rainbow colors.

First, sunlight touches a raindrop.

Next refraction occurs, resulting in bending.

The light is dispersed into seven different colors. Each color of light has a different wavelength which makes it responsible for the color.

This allows the separated colors, with their different wavelengths to reflect from the back surface of the raindrop.

A Second Refraction occurs when light exits the drop of rain. Then it retracts another time and spreads the colors.

To Look Upon a Rainbow

When the human eye views the rainbow, the droplets radiate from certain angles.

As a result, the rainbow is seen into a spectrum of seven colors, and the arc is created.

The sun and the rain work together to emanate a divine wonder!

What Do the Seven Colors Mean?

The color red displays with the longest wavelength. Various cultures view the color of red with emotions of passion and energy.

Red reminds me of the power of the blood of Jesus. Also, the color red speaks of God's protection.

When the children of Israel were about to experience the night of the 1st Passover, featuring the Destroying Angel, they were protected by the blood of a lamb.

They were instructed to place a portion of blood on their doorposts. This blood would be a sign to the Destroying Angel. Thus, the Destroying Angel would pass their household and no judgment would occur.

"The blood shall be a sign for you on (the doorposts of) the houses where you live; when I see the blood I shall pass over you, and no affliction shall happen to you to destroy you when I strike the land of Egypt" (Exodus 12: 13).

Will You Come and Pray for My House: Witchcraft is in the House?

This was a phone call that I had not expected. It was not unusual for me to receive phone calls to pray for the sick or others suffering distresses, but this was the first time I ever had someone ask me to bring a prayer team to their house and pray over the house because of witchcraft!

The mother said that the house was cursed and that noises could be heard during the night. Creaking floors and banging were some of the noises she was hearing.

I was asked to come quicky, even that very week!

The house was in the town of Speedwell, Virginia. So, I began to study about the history of the town.

Also, I prayed for the Holy Spirit to give me a strategy of prayer.

Finally, I sought the help of three other "proven" intercessors.

We prayed together as a group prior to going to the haunted house.

Quickly the day came for us to go to the haunted house! When we arrived, it was about 4 p.m. We exited our cars and were greeted by the mother. She was so excited for us to help.

We took anointing bottles of oil and applied oil to all the doors in the house.

We also applied oil on the window seals.

Then we walked around the yard and prayed over every corner of the yard.

Scriptures of protection were prayed over the house and the property.

We prayed for the protection of angels over the house. The guiding scriptures were from Psalm 91.

The whole process took us about 2 hours.

Results

After a few days, the mother followed up with me. She thanked the prayer team for coming to her house to pray.

There was a calm atmosphere in the house. There was no more banging and clanging in the night!

Peace ruled in this house, and the Holy Spirit and angels guarded their house.

Orange

The color with the next largest wavelength is orange. Several cultures and religions consider the color of orange to represent joy, enthusiasm, and creativity.

Scriptures from the Bible provide some confirmation of these meanings. The Bible relates this color with gold. Royality is associated with gold.

King Solomon was known to be wise and rich.

"*Now the weight of gold that came to Solomon in one (particular) year was six hundred and sixty-six talents of gold*" (I Kings 10: 14).

Yellow

Yellow symbolizes an atmosphere of being happy and cheerful. Yellow was a featured color for the Tabernacle built by Moses. The Tabernacle was considered a Holy Place.

"*You shall overlay the ark with pure gold, overlay it inside and out, and you shall make a gold border (frame) around its top*" (Exodus 25: 11).

Yellow was seen on the face of Moses when he came off the mountain. He had been on this mountain 40 days and nights for the purpose of receiving the Ten Commandments.

"When Moses came down from Mount Sinai with the two tablets of the Testimony in his hand, he did not know that the skin of his face was shining (with a unique radiance) because he had been speaking with God" (Exodus 34: 29).

Green

Several religions associate the color green with new growth. Nature, harmony and balance are also noted.

The Lord reveals to the Prophet Jeremiah that the man who trusts in Him will flourish like green leaves on a tree.

"For he will be (nourished) like a tree planted by the waters, That spreads out its roots by the river; and will not fear when the heat comes; But its leaves will be green and moist, And it will not be anxious and concerned in a year of drought Nor stop bearing fruit" (Jeremiah 17: 8).

Blue

The sky and the sea flash forth brilliant colors of blue. Feelings of peace and serenity are associated with this color.

Blue relates to the sapphire stone in the Bible. It is also the color of the pavement beneath God's feet.

"and they saw (a manifestation of) the God of Israel: and under His feet there appeared to be a pavement of sapphire, just as clear as the sky itself" (Exodus 24: 10).

Indigo

This is an unusual color featuring a shade between blue and violet. Insight and intuition are associated with this color.

Several cultures and religions connect this color with insight.

Ancient writings give reference to indigo dye. This dye was used for the construction of the Holy Tabernacle. It was also used in the garments of the priests.

The people were instructed by Moses to provide materials for the Tabernacle.

One such offering from the people featured goat's hair of indigo color.

"*blue, purple, and scarlet fabric, fine twisted linen, goats' hair*" (Exodus 25: 4).

Violet

The final color of the rainbow is violet. Royalty is represented by this color.

When Jesus suffered on the cross, the Romans soldiers mocked Him by placing a garment of royalty on Him.

"*They dressed Him up in (a ranking Roman officer's robe of) purple, and after twisting (together) a crown of thorns, they placed it on Him*" (Mark 15:17).

Colors of the Earthly Tabernacle

The colors of the rainbow are found in the earthly Tabernacle. The Lord instructed Moses with details for the building of the Tabernace.

A description of the Ark in found in the Book of Exodus:

"*They shall make an ark of acacia wood two and a half cubits long, one and a half cubits wide, and one and a half cubits high*" (Exodus 25:10).

The colors used for the Ark of the Covenant were ingenious and filled with rich symbolism.

The poles that carried the Ark were made of acacia wood and overlaid with gold.

Gold was a symbol for the Divine nature of God. The color of yellow is associated with gold.

Blue, purple, scarlet, and white linen were found in the inner curtains.

The divine nature of God is represented by the color blue.

Purple suggests a person of royalty.

Scarlet, which associates with red, is a symbol of the blood sacrifices. It is also a reminder of the blood of Jesus that poured from His body on the cross (Matthew 26:28).

In regards to the color of orange, it was found in the breastplate of the High Priest, in the 3rd row.

The third row contained an orange jacinth.

"*the third row a jacinth, an agate, and an amethyst*" (Exodus 28: 19).

Indigo dye was a precious substance used for construction of the holy curtains.

This dye was made from the secretion of a marine snail. The process required extracting the dye from the snail's gland. This was a tedious process to make the curtains which were positioned in holy places in the Ark.

Violet-colored dyes were used for making fabrics for the inner curtains of the Tabernacle.

The garments of the High Priests were made of white linen.

The rainbow colors were used in the following manners:

*Construction of the Ark.

*Construction of the items in the Ark.

*For making the Holy curtains.

*In the Breast-plate of the High Priest, which represented prayer intercession for the tribes.

Erection of the Tabernacle

When the Tabernacle had been completed, Moses inspected it (Exodus 40:1).

The Tabernacle (Ark) was erected with great caution, and God showed His pleasure by filling the building with His glory!

"Then the cloud (the Shekinah), God's visible, dwelling presence) covered the Tent of Meeting, and the glory and brilliance of the Lord filled the tabernacle" (Exodus 40: 34).

"Moses was not able to enter the Tent of Meeting because the cloud remained on it, and the glory and brilliance of the Lord filled the tabernacle" (Exodus 40: 35).

Meeting Place Between God and Man

In the Tabernacle a meeting place for God and the High Priest was constructed. This would be a holy place, that only the High Priest could enter.

Only once a year could the High Priest enter, and his duty was to present atonement offerings for the nation.

Two cherubim, angelic figures, stood above the mercy seat. Their wings were stretched out, and touched each other in the center.

"You shall make two cherubim (winged angelic figures) of (solid) hammered gold at the ends of the mercy seat" (Exodus 25:18).

"Make one cherub at each end, making the cherubim of one piece with the mercy seat at its two ends" (Exodus 25:19).

"The cherubim shall have their wings spread upward, covering the mercy seat with their wings and facing each other. The faces of the cherubim are to be looking downward toward the mercy seat."

"You shall have the mercy seat on the top of the ark, and in the ark you will put the Testimony which I will give you" (Exodus 25: 21).

This majestic meeting place was treated with great reverence by the priests and the people.

When God appeared, the Shekinah Glory of God was seen as a thick, visible cloud. This fiery cloud also led the Israelites in the wilderness.

At times the Presence of the Cloud was so thick that even Moses could not stand up to minister to the Lord!

The New Testament Begins

When Jesus died on the cross, the heavy veil of the Temple was torn.

This was a divine message from God!

Mankind now had access to the Throne of God. They did not need a High Priest to go before them.

In repentance and prayer, man could approach the Living God.

Jesus was now the High Priest for all who would acknowledge Him, and Jesus served in the Heavenly Temple.

"But as it is, Christ has acquired a (priestly) ministry which is more excellent (than the old Levitical priestly ministry), for He is the Mediator (Arbiter) of a better covenant (uniting God and man), which has been enacted and rests on better promises" (Hebrews 8: 6).

The Temple is Seen in Heaven

For those who wonder what heaven is like, all they need to do is read Revelation Chapter 4.

Apostle John was given a heavenly invitation and experienced the joy of being in heaven.

"At once I was in (special communication with) the Spirit; and behold, a throne stood in heaven, with One seated on the throne" (Revelation 4:2).

It is significant that the first thing John saw was a symbol of authority. Heaven was ruled and protected by God!

He saw the Throne and He that sat upon the throne.

This teaches us that Heaven has a system and a structure of divine authority.

"And He who sat there appeared like (the crystalline sparkle) of a jasper stone and (the

fiery redness of) a sardius stone, and ENRCIRCLING THE THRONE there was a rainbow that looked like (the color of an) emerald" (Revelation 4: 3).

During His time on earth, Jesus demonstrated the authority of Heaven.

He even taught His disciples to pray, "*Thy Kingdom Come, Thy will be Done*" (Matthew 6:6 -13).

Our prayers should reflect the authority of God!

*Pray in His Name, for it has authority!

*Let prayers be made to acknowledge the power of the Blood of Jesus! (Revelation 12:11).

*Pray verses from the Word of God, for His Word is power! (Hebrews 4:12).

The people were amazed at the authority of Jesus when He preached and when He prayed.

"and they were surprised (almost overwhelmed) at His teaching, because His message was (given) with authority and power and great ability" (Luke 4: 32).

The demons also recognized His authority!

"Demons also were coming out of many people, shouting, "You are the

Son of God!" But He rebuked them and would not allow them to speak, because they knew that He was the Christ (the Messiah, the Anointed)" (Luke 4: 41).

Likewise, the disciples would experience this divine authority.

"The seventy returned with joy, saying, Lord, even the demons are subject to us in Your Name" (Luke 10: 17).

Jesus confirmed that this authority would be given to His followers!

"Listen carefully; I have given you authority (that you now possess) to tread on serpents and

scorpions, and (the ability to exercise the authority) over all the power of the enemy (Satan): and nothing will (in any way) harm you" (Luke 10: 19).

The Authority of the Rainbow

Notice that the rainbow encircling the throne is mentioned in the same verse which describes the throne (Revelation 4:3).

Truly, this rainbow is a symbol of authority.

When the Great Red Dragon sees this RAINBOW, he knows that God's authority is superior. He knows that he cannot touch God's Throne or God's people who have embraced the protection of the rainbow encircling the Throne of God!

"Then I heard a loud voice in heaven, saying,

"Now the salvation, and the power, and the kingdom (dominion, reign) of our God, and the authority of His Christ have come: for the

accuser of our (believing) brothers and sisters has been thrown down (at last),he who accuses them and keeps bringing charges (of sinful behavior) against them before our God day and night" (Revelation 12: 10).

Reflection Questions

1. List three ways that the rainbow speaks of victory for God's people. (Genesis 6 and Revelation 4)

2. What is your favorite color of the rainbow?

3. What promises of God does your favorite color symbolize?

4. How is God's authority revealed through the rainbow?

5. What message does the rainbow surrounding God's throne send to the Great Red Dragon?

CHAPTER 3: THE RAINBOW STANDS BETWEEN GOD'S THRONE AND THE GREAT READ DRAGON

BETWEEN is a word of war for the saints of God. Several times the scriptures reveal that God stands between the enemy and His people in a protective manner.

One of the most confirming examples is seen by His pillar of cloud by day, and fire by night.

"The angel of God, who had been going in front of the camp of Israel, moved and went behind them, the pillar of cloud moved from in front and stood behind them."

So, it came BETWEEN the camp of Egypt and the camp of Israel. It was a cloud along with darkness (even by day to the Egyptians), but it gave light by night (to the Israelites); so one (army) did not come near the other all night" (Exodus 14: 19,20).

Just imagine the rainbow surrounding God's Throne, flashing brilliant colors of light!

It reminds the forces of darkness that they cannot advance against God's Kingdom.

Also, lightning and thunder are emitted from the throne, which also sent a message to the enemy.

"From the throne came flashes of lightning and (rumbling) sounds and peals of thunder. Seven lamps of fire were burning in front of the

throne; which are the seven Spirits of God;"
(Revelation 4:5).

The Position of an Intercessor

Even as the rainbow is close to God's
Throne, the intercessor should be positioned
close to God.

*"Come close to God (with a contrite heart),
and He will come close to you. Wash your
hands, you sinners; and purify your
(unfaithful) hearts, you double-minded
(people)* (James 4:8).

I Found His Presence at the Altar

I truly appreciated the opportunities to
approach the altar and pray.

There was a church that strongly encouraged
us to spend personal time at the altar at each
service.

I recall those moments of crying out to God for a touch of His presence and I was not disappointed!

Many times, the heavens would open for me. The Holy Spirit blew over me in strong waves. His peace covered my heart, and the burdens that I brought to the altar were noticed by heaven. Very often I would stand up from the altar and see prayers answered, even the same day!

I saw family members accept Jesus as Lord!

I saw bodies healed!

I saw money come!

I saw job opportunities open up for me and my family!

I saw difficult problems resolved!

I saw God in action because I obeyed His command to, "Come."

In Heavenly Places

The successful intercessor quickly learns that our battles are not with flesh and blood, but with evil spirits in the heavenlies.

"For our struggle is not against flesh and blood (contending only with physical opponents), but against the world forces of this (present) darkness, against spiritual forces of wickedness in the heavenly (supernatural) places" (Ephesians 6: 12).

The Rainbow is positioned in **HIGH PLACES**. Therefore, it is seen by heaven, earth and the spiritual realm. This position gives it power!

Our prayers should be prayed from high places. That means we must come boldly to the Throne of God.

"And He has raised us up together with Him (when we believed), and seated us with Him

in the heavenly places, (because we are) in Christ Jesus" (Ephesians 2 6).

This position of prayer sets the Christian intercessors apart from all other religions that encourage prayers.

Come to the Throne of God. Come with the qualifications given us by Jesus Christ.

"*Therefore let us (with privilege) approach the throne of grace (that is, the throne of God's gracious favor) with confidence and without fear, so that we may receive mercy (for our failures) and find (His amazing grace to help in time of need (an appropriate blessing, coming just at the right moment*" (Hebrews 4: 16).

Rainbow Prayers

Even as the rainbow surrounds the throne of God, we must surround ourselves and families with the promises of God's Word!

We do this by praying scripture verses over our situations.

Embrace the colors of the rainbow, by praying the prayers associated with each color!

Red

Recall that red is the color with the longest wavelength. The color of red symbolizes passion, love and courage for many cultures.

With great passion and courage, Jesus Christ died on the cross so we could have eternal life and be delivered from evil.

His blood also gives us the privilege to enter into the heavenly places with prayers.

"Therefore, believers, since we have confidence and full freedom to enter the Holy Place (the place where God dwells) by (means of) the blood of Jesus" (Hebrews 10: 19).

The blood of Jesus also gives us the victory of overcoming the devil (Revelation 12: 11).

PRAYER: Father, In the Name of Jesus, I appreciate the precious blood of Jesus. I repent of my sins as instructed by I John 1:9.

I receive forgiveness of my sins, and the promise of no condemnation.

The enemy that distresses me is defeated, for I overcome by the blood of Jesus!

Orange

The color of orange reflects enthusiasm and endurance. In the scriptures, this color is associated with God's fire and Divine Presence.

The question for intercessors is, "Do you welcome God's Presence in your times of prayer?"

Without God's Presence, what value could be placed upon prayer?

The Book of Song of Solomon challenges us to welcome His Presence.

"Let me see your face,

Let me hear your voice;

For your voice is sweet,

And your face is lovely." (Song of Solomon 2: 14)

PRAYER: Father, In the Name of Jesus, I ask for a fresh encounter with Your Divine Presence.

Let me see your face,

Let me hear your voice;

For your voice is sweet,

And Your face is lovely.

Fill me with Your joy, peace and power. Fill me with courage and strength. Lead me this day and night.

Yellow

Because yellow is associated with gold, it represents God's divine presence.

Yellow is a color also symbolizing understanding and spiritual enlightenment.

"*In Your Light, we see Light*" (Psalm 36: 9).

PRAYER: Father, In the Name of Jesus give light to my concerns. I need answers to difficult questions. Shine your light upon me and reveal heavenly solutions.

Green

The Bible references green to new life and growth.

It also suggests a time for new beginnings.

Green is a reminder that we must grow in our faith.

King David refers to his spiritual condition as a green olive tree.

"But as for me, I am like a green olive tree in the house of God" (Psalm 52: 8).

PRAYER: Father, In the Name of Jesus, revive me in areas of my life where I have become stagnant.

Revive my spirit. Renew my hope and faith.

Revive lost dreams and hopes.

Give life to my future.

Blue

Blue is a color that reminds us of God's heavenly realm. The blue skies speak of His wisdom.

Blue symbolizes wisdom. Two people known for their wisdom were Daniel and King Solomon.

It was wisdom that delivered Daniel from the den of lions.

Wisdom can also deliver us from difficult situations.

PRAYER: Father, in the Name of Jesus, I ask for wisdom for the situations that I face.

The wisdom of God is much better than the answers of man.

Answer me, with Your wisdom.

Show me the answers and solutions for the problems I face.

Indigo

Since indigo is close to the color of blue, it also symbolizes wisdom.

Royalty is also associated with indigo.

It is important for us to know that we belong to God.

"It is He that has made us, not we ourselves (and we are His), We are the sheep of His pasture" (Psalm 100: 3).

PRAYER: Father, in the Name of Jesus, I acknowledge that I belong to You.

Help me to know You and Your ways. Help me to please You.

Help me to bring honor to Your Name!

Violet

Violet is associated with royalty and priesthood.

This color was used for parts of the Holy Tabernacle and for the garments of the High Priest.

It was the duty of the priests to represent the people to God.

The priests were to pray for the people, and lead them in the ways of God.

PRAYER: Father, in the Name of Jesus, help me to have the character of divine royalty.

Help me to live with high moral standards.

Help me to stand as an intercessor for the needs of others.

The Seven Spirits Before the Throne of God

There are seven colors in the rainbow which surrounds God's Throne.

There are also Seven Spirits around the Throne.

"From the Throne came flashes of lightning and (rumbling) sounds and peals of thunder. Seven lamps of fire were burning in front of the throne, which are the seven Spirit of God."

The Prophet Isaiah reveals these seven spirits.

These are the Spirits that rested upon Jesus.

*The Spirit of the Lord

*The Spirit of Wisdom

*The Spirit of Understanding

*The Spirit of Counsel

*The Spirit of Might

*The Spirit of Knowledge

*The Spirit of the fear of the Lord

(Isaiah 11: 1-5)

Reflection Questions

God wants to shine His love, life and light through you (Matthew 5: 16).

1. Will you embrace the colors of the rainbow and allow God to shine through you?

2. How is this performed? Example: praying with a needy soul.
3. When we spend time on a daily basis with God in prayer and study of His Word, we receive more of His Light!
4. When we show love and compassion to others, we share His Light!

CLOSING PRAYER

Heavenly Father,

We bow before Your throne, where the rainbow shines with eternal brilliance, reminding us of Your covenant of mercy and Your promise of protection. Thank You that when You look upon the rainbow, You remember Your people, and when we look upon it, we remember that Your Word cannot fail.

Lord, we understand that the Red Dragon still rages, but we rejoice that he has been defeated. By the blood of Jesus Christ, by the power of Your Word, and by the authority of Your Spirit, the enemy is silenced and his schemes are undone. We stand in victory today because the Lamb has overcome, and we belong to Him.

Father, let the colors of the rainbow surround our lives. Let the red remind us of the blood of Jesus, our covering and our deliverance. Let the orange burn with the fire of Your presence and the endurance of Your Spirit. Let the yellow shine as Your light, giving wisdom and revelation to our hearts. Let the green declare new life, growth, and fruitfulness in every season. Let the blue lift our eyes to heaven, filling us with peace and divine wisdom. Let the indigo remind us that we are Yours, a royal priesthood, called and chosen. Let the violet clothe us in the dignity of Your kingdom, standing as intercessors for our families, our nation, and the world.

Surround us, Lord, as You surrounded Israel with a pillar of cloud by day and fire by night. Let the sevenfold Spirit rest upon us—the Spirit of the Lord, of wisdom, of understanding, of counsel, of might, of knowledge, and of the fear of the Lord. Clothe us with the armor of God, that we may resist the devil and see him flee. Teach us to pray with the authority of Jesus, who stilled storms and rebuked the enemy with the power of Your Word.

Create in us clean hearts, O God, and renew steadfast spirits within us. Let our lives be a testimony to Your faithfulness. May our prayers rise before You like incense, and may the sound of our worship echo the songs of angels who cry, "Holy, holy, holy, is the Lord God Almighty."

Until that day when we see You face to face, and the rainbow of Your throne fills our sight with glory, keep us faithful. Keep us watchful. Keep us victorious!

We give You all honor, all praise, and all glory.

In the mighty name of Jesus Christ, the King of kings and Lord of lords, we pray.

Amen.